HE'S King OF KINGS

by **MOSIE LISTER**

Narrations by **KEN BIBLE**

A Musical Worshiping the Christ of Christmas

FROM THE **EASY 2 EXCEL** SERIES

Lillenas PUBLISHING COMPANY

Kansas City, MO 64141

CONTENTS

Joy!

Joyfully ♩ = ca. 104

Arranged by Mosie Lister

*"Joy to the World"

Men and Sopranos sing upper part
Altos sing lower part

Joy to the world! the Lord is come; Let

earth re- ceive her King._____ Let

6

The glo‑ries of His righ‑teous‑ness, And

won‑ders of His love, And won‑ders of His love, And
And won‑ders of His love, and won‑ders of His

CD: 3

won‑ders, won‑ders of His love.
love and

*"Give Your Voice to the Wind"
2-part choir

O give your voice to the wind as all the heav‑ens be‑gin to

praise Him. Lift your hearts to the skies while all cre‑

No Room?

Underscore

MOSIE LISTER

*Narrator: Joy to the world! The Lord *has* come. Let earth received her King!
But the reception He got that night long ago was anything but royal.

*Narrator begins

Gently ♩ = ca. 69

CD: 5

When Mary and Joseph arrived in Bethlehem, weary from a long
journey, the town found no place for them and for the newborn Savior.

A dingy stable was His castle. The animals were his royal court.
And the manger, a feeding trough full of hay, was his only throne.

Bethlehem, you were honored as the birthplace of the King of Kings.
Your God came to you that night, just like He promised. Why weren't
you expecting Him? Why didn't you know Him when He came?

O Bethlehem

Solo

Words and Music by
MOSIE LISTER
Arranged by Mosie Lister

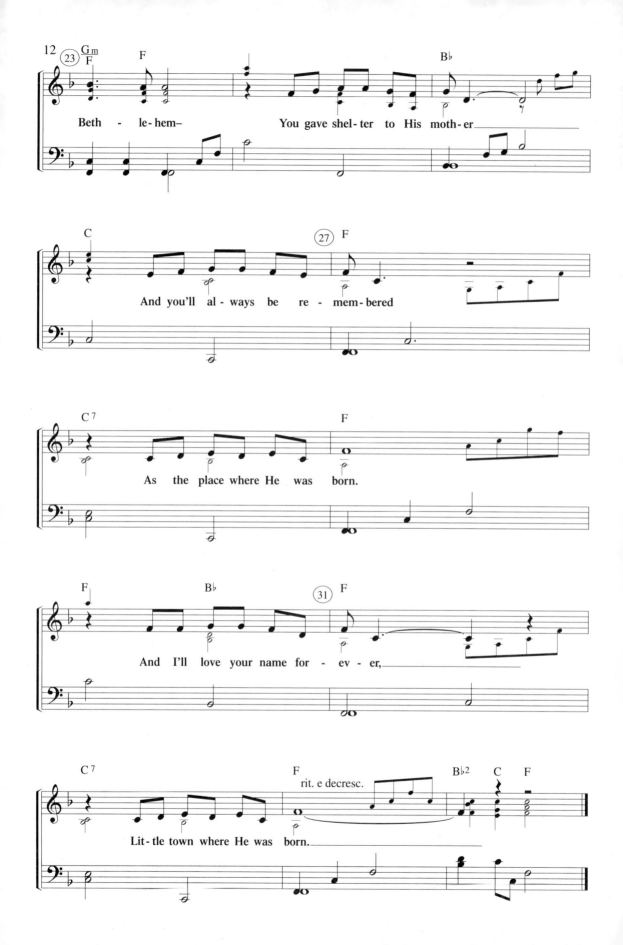

Rejoice!
Underscore

MOSIE LISTER

Majestic ♩ = ca. 88

CD: 9

*NARRATOR: To us a Child is born, to us a Son is given,

*Narrator begins

cresc.

And the government will be on His shoulders. And He will be called

Wonderful Counselor, Mighty God, Everlasting Father, Prince of Peace *(Isaiah 9:6, NIV)*

Baby Boy

Optional Children's Choir

Arranged by Mosie Lister

*"What Was the Name of the Baby Boy?"

1. What was the name of the ba - by boy?
2. Born in a sta - ble, so I've been told.

What was the name of the ba - by boy?
Born in a sta - ble, so I've been told.

What was the name of the ba - by boy
Born in a sta - ble, so I've been told,

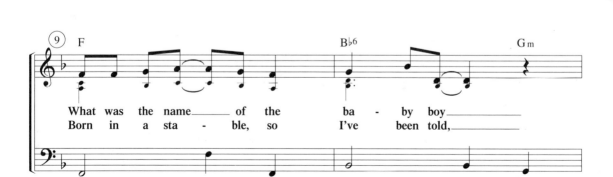

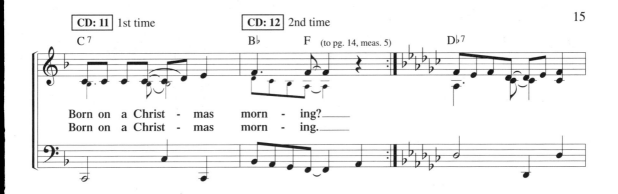

(to pg. 14, meas. 5)

Born on a Christ - mas morn - ing?____
Born on a Christ - mas morn - ing.____

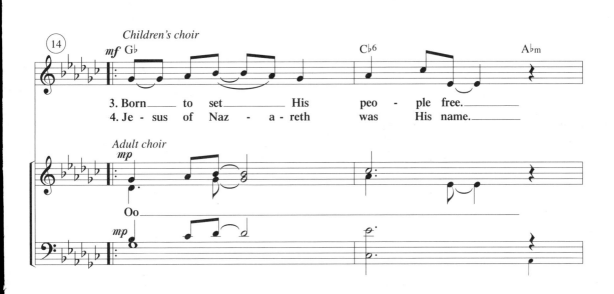

Children's choir

3. Born____ to set____ His peo - ple free.____
4. Je - sus of Naz - a - reth was His name.____

Adult choir

Oo____

Born____ to set____ His peo - ple free.____
Je - sus of Naz - a - reth was His name.____

Oo____

18

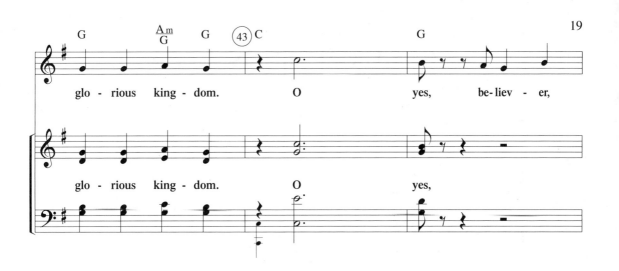

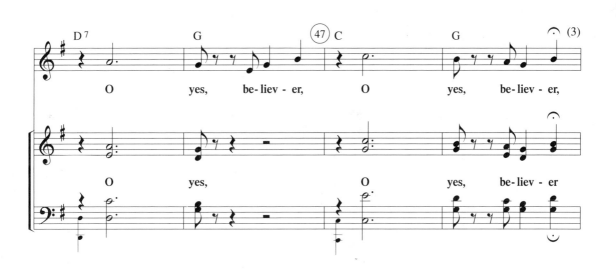

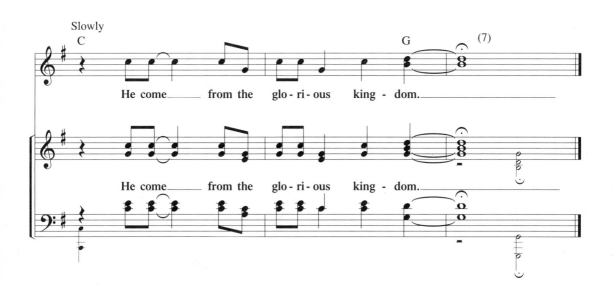

The Shepherds

Underscore

MOSIE LISTER

Brightly ♩. = ca. 72

CD: 17

*Narrator begins (1st time)

*NARRATOR: There were shepherds living out in the fields nearby, keeping watch over

their flocks by night. An angel of the Lord appeared to them, and the glory of the Lord
shone around them, and they were terrified.

But the angel said to them, "Do not be afraid. I bring you good news of great joy that
will be for all the people. Today in the town of David a Savior has been born to you;

He is Christ the Lord. This will be a sign to you: You will find a baby wrapped in cloths and lying in a manger."

Suddenly a great company of the heavenly host appeared with the angel, praising God

and saying, "Glory to God in the highest, and on earth peace to men on whom His favor rests." *(Luke 2:8-14, NIV)*

King of Kings
Optional Congregational Participation

Arranged by Mosie Lister

*"Angels We Have Heard on High"

24

Jesus, the Son of God

KEN BIBLE and
G. T. HAYWOOD

G. T. HAYWOOD
Arranged by Mosie Lister

Your Name Is Wonderful

Underscore

MOSIE LISTER

Stately ♩ = ca. 76

*NARRATOR: Jesus, our Lord, how majestic is Your name in all the earth!
You have set Your glory above the heavens.

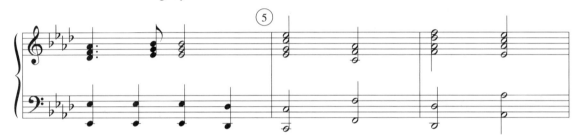

Even from the lips of children You bring forth honor and blessing and praise.

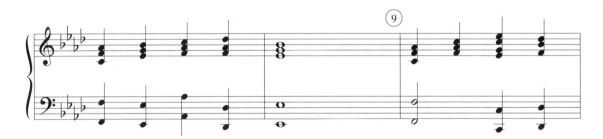

O Lord, our Lord, Mighty God, Everlasting Father, Prince of Peace, Your name is Wonderful!
(Adapted from Psalm 8:1-2; Isa. 9:6)

O Lord, How Wonderful

MOSIE LISTER
and KEN BIBLE

MOSIE LISTER
Arranged by Mosie Lister

He's Still the King of Kings

GLORIA GAITHER, WILLIAM J. GAITHER
and RONN HUFF

WILLIAM J. GAITHER
Arranged by Mosie Lister

All of Me

Underscore

MOSIE LISTER

CD: 34 Smoothly ♩ = ca. 80

*NARRATOR: He's still the King of Kings and Lord of Lords.

*Narrator begins

Yet He humbled Himself. He made Himself nothing. Though He was the eternal God, He
took on the form of a servant. He became obedient, even to the point of death.

Of all the wonders we celebrate at Christmas, this is the one I find most moving. Jesus Christ

left the peace and the holiness of heaven. He set aside all that He had. And He came to me.

He Came

with
He Came to Me
Thou Didst Leave Thy Throne

Arranged by Mosie Lister

45 *"Thou Didst Leave Thy Throne"

Give Your Voice to the Wind

with
Joy to the World

Words and Music by
MOSIE LISTER and KEN BIBLE
Arranged by Mosie Lister

NARRATOR: *(without music)* Joy to the world! The Lord is come. Let earth receive her King! Let every heart prepare Him room And heaven and nature sing!

CD: 39

46